Happy Harlow
The Tail of an Emotional Support Dog

Happy Harlow
Copyright © 2021 by Jordyn Croft

All rights reserved. No part of this publication may be reproduced, distributed, or transmitted in any form or by any means, including photocopying, recording, or other electronic or mechanical methods, without the prior written permission of the author, except in the case of brief quotations embodied in critical reviews and certain other non-commercial uses permitted by copyright law.

Tellwell Talent
www.tellwell.ca

ISBN
978-0-2288-6240-6 (Hardcover)
978-0-2288-6239-0 (Paperback)

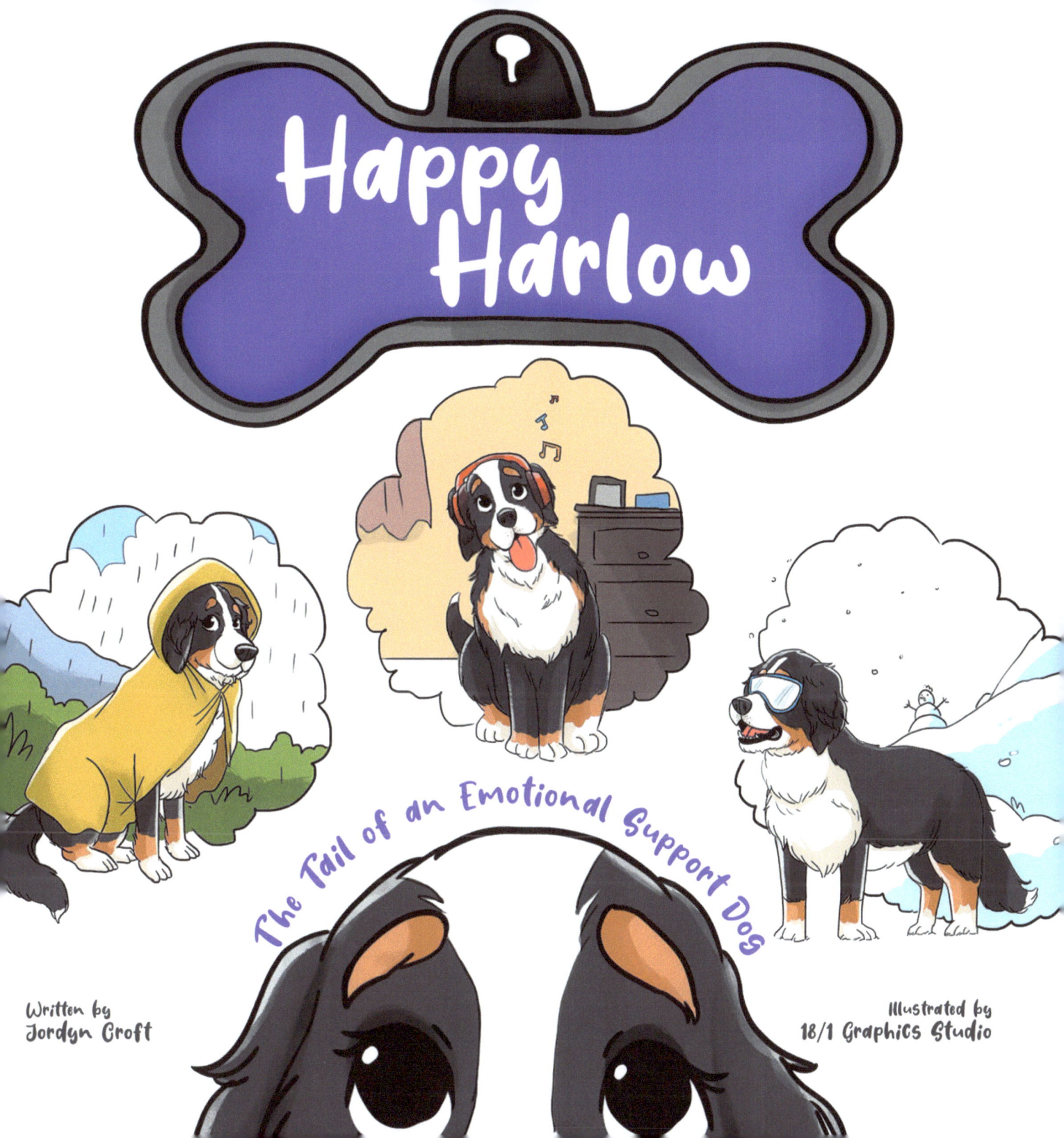

Dedication:

To Christina Dawn Ives, the woman who gave me the dog that has enhanced my quality of life immensely, and to my mother for encouraging me to share that dog's story.

Acknowledgements:

This book would not be out in the world without the support and funding from various people including friends, family, friends of family, and my community. Thank you.

My name is Harlow and I am so happy!
I am so happy because I have a very special job.

When I am full of energy, we go to the dog park so I can run around with other dogs and sniff everything!
This helps me stay focused when we go to special places.

My human and I go all kinds of special places together. I'm always ready and waiting by the door for our next adventure!

We go to the doctors to get check-ups on sick days!

I am even allowed to go to work with my human.

She works at a school and I get to play with all the kids there!

I think I like when we go to restaurants best because I usually get a special snack.

I love meeting new people everywhere I go.
I have made so many special friends.

I love when I get to spend special break time alone with my human too. Our favourite thing to do together is lay in our hammock.

© Jordyn Montana Croft 2021

In loving memory

www.ingramcontent.com/pod-product-compliance
Lightning Source LLC
LaVergne TN
LVHW071653060526
838200LV00029B/446